Ottoman Sounds

BOYUT MUSIC
BOYUT PUBLISHING GROUP

Ceo
Bülent ÖZÜKAN

General Manager
Nilgün ÖZÜKAN

General Art Director
Murat ÖNEŞ

Supervisor
Gönül PAÇACI

English Edition
Mısra Öncel

Translation
Atilla Eröncel

Art Director
Yıldız Ertan

Graphic Design
Şehnaz Çekcen
Ümit Vurgun
Şebnem Akgöl

Electronic Publishing Coordinator
Çağatay Özgür

ISBN 975-521-434-8

₿
BOYUT PUBLISHING GROUP

Matbaacılar Sitesi No: 115, 34560
BAĞCILAR / ISTANBUL
Tel: +90 212 629 53 00 (pbx)
Faks: +90 212 629 05 74-75

e-mail:info@boyut.com.tr

www.boyut.com.tr

This edition published by
Boyut Publishing Group Istanbul / TURKEY

MAGNIFICENT
Ottoman
Composers

Ottoman

It is necessary to state at the outset the difficulty of getting to know the creators of Ottoman music through limited biographical knowledge and through their works which have undergone changes both qualitatively and quantitatively over the years. If one remembers that it has been only a little over a hundred years since sounds could be put into written notes, then one can understand the impossibility of getting to know this music on a one-to-one basis and to note the changes that have taken place over time. It is possible to have some idea about them through some written documents that have survived and the forms that they have taken through the meşk which is a verbal method of passing down music from master to apprecentice. The studies and performances that are done with today's understanding and interpretation can only give us a limited idea about their original and pure quality. For that reason, it is necessary to remember some of the fundamental and distinguishing peculiarities of Ottoman music.

Ottoman music, just like Ottoman literature, architecture and calligraphy, is a composite product of the upper strata of Ottoman society. The original structure of the civilization created by the Ottomans provides the foundation for the creation of music. The architectural works, miniature works, calligraphy and similar visual arts, along with literary works, are elements that have come into being in different art forms which represent a parallelism with each other and complete each other.

Generally speaking, this music which has developed within the strictures of Eastern culture and within the literary culture has an original construction and within this construction has original details such as usul and makam.

Its creation, transmittal and teaching has undergone many changes up to the present and it was only possible to put it into written notes after many

Sounds

various attempts. If one remembers that it was only toward the middle of the 19th century in the West that the use of written notes was adopted that one can understand the changes in these works which up until then had only been passed down through memory.

Therefore, we are faced with a totality of works that continually changed in form and style after they were created, and on the other hand we are faced with a dynamic participation that caused these changes. Special sounds that are used in Ottoman music which are called perde, unequal spacing between notes, a linear melodic construction and rich rhythmical substance are characteristics that give the first impression. This music, which had been composed, performed and taught without being written down, is now confined to notes and certain forms and this is the fundamental difference in our understanding of this music. After having made this determination, we can say that the understanding that the changes in form and technique have made are secondary and natural developments. Just like the changes in society, this music, which has a past of 600 years, has come to the present day by carrying this tradition from generation to generation. It is necessary to point out that composers who are discussed in "Ottoman Sounds" are different stars that shine in different parts of this universe. It is up to listeners to see and sense the area of illumination of all these stars which are commensurate with the power and distance of these stars. The information given about the lives of these composers which was obtained from reliable sources is not just their life stories but the cultural and artistic environment in which they lived and the places that they occupy in this musical tradition and their understanding of music.

Buhûrî-zâde Mustafa Efendi

Itrî

1640? - 1712

Magnificent Ottoman Composers

Buhûrî-zâde Mustafa Efendi (Itrî)

He is an important composer of Turkish classical music or Ottoman music at a time when the rules of music had become mature. Historian İsmail Hakkı Uzunçarşılı in his book "Musical Life in the Palace During the Ottoman Times," after stating that palace musical life that was developed in the 17th century continued in the 18th century gives the following information pertaining to the period in which Itri lived:

"We see quite a number of good composers in the 17th century which is a direct result of the interest in music shown by music-loving Sultans Mehmet IV and Ahmet IV. Among these who had relations with the palace and whose works were performed in the presence of the Sultans and appreciated by them were Kadıasker İbrahim Efendi, Hafız Post, Tanburi Mehmet Efendi, Buhuri-zade Mustafa Itri, Ama Kadri, Hoca Osman Efendi, Recep Çelebi, Küçük Müezzin Mehmet Çelebi, Küçük İmam.

According to Itrî R.

An innovative soul, seeking to break the cliche away

e was born in Istanbul near Mevlanakapı in a section known as Yaylak. His name is Mustafa and because of his father's occupation he came to be known as Buhuri-zade. In all sources one can find, he is listed as the greatest composer of Turkish classical music as well as religious music. His life spanned the reigns of five sultans. These are: Mehmet IV (1648–1687), Süleyman II (1687-1691), Ahmed II (1691-1695), Mustafa II (1695-1703) and Ahmed III (1703-1730). He was variously known as Hanende Buhuri-zade (singer), Mustafa Çelebi Muallim-i Enderun-i Humayun (Teacher of the Royal School), Mustafa Çelebi Buhuri-zade Hanende-i Harem-i Humayun (Royal Harem Singer) and finally he was appointed Head of the Slave Traders.

In many sources, it is concluded that he had a solid education judging by his poems and musical compositions. He especially enjoyed the concern and protection of Sultan Mehmet IV and the ruler of Crimea, Selim Giray. Rauf Yekta Bey who has written the first and most extensive study on Itri, published originally in the Tevhidi-i Efkar (Union of Thoughts) newspaper and later in "Mevlevi Ayınleri (Whirling Dervish Rites) serial at the Istanbul Conservatory of Music has made the following observation. "In the works of composers prior to Itri, the Iranian influence is evident, as it is indeed evident in literature. Itri was able to eliminate this influence completely and has the honor of creating a pure Turkish music style."

Sultan Mehmet IV.
(1648-1687)

Ahmed II.
(1691-1695)

Süleyman II.
(1687-1691)

Mustafa II.
(1695-1703)

Ahmet III.
(1703-1730)

The best
composer of
Turkish Classical
Music, Itrî lived during
era of 5 sultans the
sovereignty history had been written.

دار الالحان كلّيّاتی

نومرو

٢٥ – ٢٤

نوا مقام ندن كلّ

بيرنفیلّ ايقاعنده

نوا مرّبّع

انجليز ايقاعنده

دار الالحانده منتشكل هيئت علميه طرفندن تدقيق و قبول ايدلمشدر

هر حقّی محفوظ طدر

فياتی ١٠ فرشده

مطبعهٔ عثمانيه

An example of musical notes
named Dâru'l Elhán Külliyah.

12

In fact, looking at the period prior to him, for instance the works that are attributed to Abdülkadır Meragi, the difference can be noted immediately in melodic construction and style. In his youth he regularly attended the Yenikapı Dervish Lodge and was influenced by many of the masters at the lodge, particularly the sheikh of the period, Cami Ahmed Dede. It is also stated that he too was a mevlevi and played the ney. However, there is no information with regard to any other education that he received other than the dervish lodge. Most of the sources referred to the perfection of his singing and the depth of his knowledge of music. Evliya Çelebi in his "Book of Travels" (Seyahatname) refers to him as "a master of composition, a mature honorable expert." It is known that Itri, some of whose poems have survived to this day, also received a diploma from Siyahi Ahmet Efendi in the Persian style of calligraphy. Using the nom de plume, Itri in his poems, he wrote muamma, gazel, tarih and kıta, in various magazines and chronicles. He even wrote some türküs using syllabic rhyme. However it is known that at the time that Itri lived, there were two other men named Buhuri-zade. Therefore it is necessary to be very careful when doing research.

It is said that his music teacher was Hafız Post the most famous and masterful composer of his time. Historian, Yılmaz Öztuna, thinks that this is a strong possibility because several lines that Itri had added to a handwritten music text magazine put out by Post clearly shows the similarity of the two men's musical understanding and the style in their works. Furthermore, Saadettin Nüzhet Ergun in the section on the 18th century of his religious music encyclopedia mentions the possibility that he might have learned music from famous people of the time: Koca Osman and Dervish Ömer. Itri wrote chronograms for these three composers and another musician known as Kücük İmam.

Buhûrî-zâde Mustafa Efendi (Itrî)

Even though very few of his works have survived to the present, Itri because of his works that reflect the musical understanding of this period, his mastery of other forms of art, his relations with other musical masters, and his influence on his contemporaries and followers, has a unique place in the history of Turkish music. During the reign of Murat IV he served as the head singer of the palace chorus, was a courtier to the Sultan, was a music teacher to the concubines in the royal harem and was a music teacher at the Palace School.

Finally he asked the Sultan, who was a great admirer of Itri, for the job of Steward of Slave Traders. This was accepted and he remained in this position until the end of his life. It is thought that the reason he chose this job was because he wanted to select young female slaves with good voices and an affinity for music and even to listen to the music from different parts of the world. On the basis of various magazines and memoranda and a

poetic line giving the date of his death, it is calculated that he died in 1711 or 1712. It is not known where he is buried. Aside from the information given by Şeyh that he was buried outside the Yenikapı Dervish Lodge there is no certain information other than rumors.

The date of birth of Itrî is unknown but he's died on 1124 in Edirnekapı.

However this is a controversial maller, in Kocamustafapaşa a tomb was found and confirmed as his tomb.

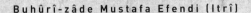

Masterpieces...
The Work of a Genius

İtri is a composer shown as an example of a composer who composed many works but with only a few surviving to the present. Although it is rumored and reported that he had over a thousand compositions, Suphi Ezgi in Atrab ül Asar (The Joys of Relic) gives the following information: "Even though in his biography we stated that his works number more than one thousand, according to Esad Efendi, this number is well over two thousand." However this information serves no other purpose than to show the magnitude of the loss.

In the end, the number of works that have survived, although many think that this is around twenty, actually is around forty. Ten of these are examples of religious Sufi music, the others are instrumental music, kar, beste, ağır and yürük semai. It is necessary to point out that his works that have survived to our day are capable of giving us enough information about his music. He left his imprint on the period in which he lived and earned the title of Hoca. Rauf Yekta Bey says that there is no doubt that these works that have survived the trepidations of centuries are the true classics of Turkish music. This is a very astute observation when one considers that this repertoire was only put into notes toward the end of the 19th century.

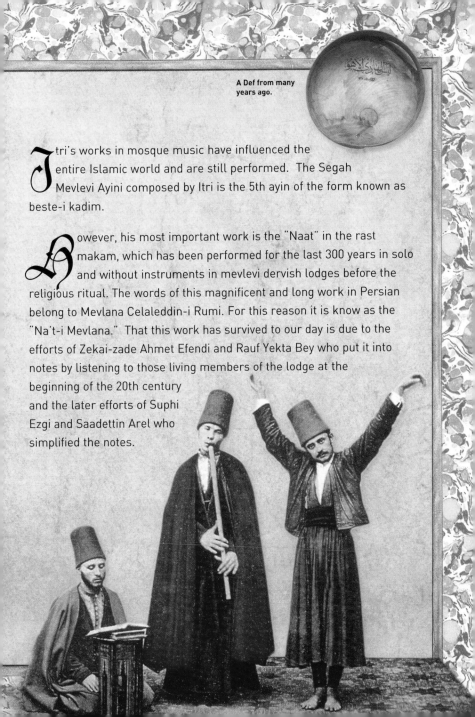

A Def from many years ago.

Itri's works in mosque music have influenced the entire Islamic world and are still performed. The Segah Mevlevi Ayini composed by Itri is the 5th ayin of the form known as beste-i kadim.

However, his most important work is the "Naat" in the rast makam, which has been performed for the last 300 years in solo and without instruments in mevlevi dervish lodges before the religious ritual. The words of this magnificent and long work in Persian belong to Mevlana Celaleddin-i Rumi. For this reason it is know as the "Na't-i Mevlana." That this work has survived to our day is due to the efforts of Zekai-zade Ahmet Efendi and Rauf Yekta Bey who put it into notes by listening to those living members of the lodge at the beginning of the 20th century and the later efforts of Suphi Ezgi and Saadettin Arel who simplified the notes.

The most famous and artful secular of his works is the Neva Kar, the words of which belong to Şirazlı Hafız. This long work, unanimously hailed as a work of genius, goes through many makams and styles and uses all forms of composition technique. It is considered the masterpiece of Turkish musical repertoire which has influenced not only the musical world but also literary people from Tanpınar to Yahya Kemal. Necil Kazım Akses, one of the composers of Western music in the Republic, wrote a scherzo based on this work.

There is still a chance to find other works of Itri through new research. E. R. Üngör added some of his poems after going through old documents to his publication "Güfte Antoloji" (Anthology of Musical Text). Through the collections in the archives that have not been organized, it may still be possible to find other works of Itri's along with their notes. Ruştu Şardağ in a book he published in 1989 was able to find some of Itri's poems in a collection belonging to the 17th century. Even though Itri composed in almost all forms of Turkish music including short songs and türküs, some of his secular works that have survived to this day: Bayâtî, Rehâvî, Nühüft peşrev and Nühüft instrumental semai; Pençgâh, Bestenigâr, Bayâtî, Nikriz, Buselik, Rehâvî, Isfahan, Hisar, Uşşak bestes; Irak, Nühüft, Hisar, Segâh, Isfahan ağır semâis.

İSTANBUL
KONSERVATUVARI

NEŞRİYATI

Türk Musikisinin Klasikleri

№ 167

BUHURI ZADE

MUSTAFA ITRİ EFENDİ

PENCÜGÂH MURABBA
FERİ İKAİNDA

KONSERVATUVARDAKİ İLMİ HEY'ET TARAFINDAN
TETKİK ve KABUL EDİLMİŞTİR.
HER HAKKI MAHFUZDUR

FİATI 5 KURUŞ

Itrî - Nevâ Kâr and Yahyâ Kemâl

Of the Itri concert that was given by the Turkish Music Performance Ensemble of the Istanbul Municipality Conservatory, Halil Can, a valuable ney player and member of the Conservatory Organization Board, said the following, "In our music, when we think of Yahya Kemal, the first thing that comes to our mind is the great composer Itri. Whenever we speak of Itri we remember his Neva Kar and his other masterpieces. Whenever the neva makam is mentioned, the first work again belongs to Itri. There are two reasons why the great poet was so enamored with Neva Kar; the words belong to the famous Hafız of Shiraz (who died 1791 1388). His real name is Mehmed Şemsüddin. He was born in 1720 (1320). There is a close resemblance between Hafız's nature, his disposition and his poesy, and that of Yahya Kemal's. This is number one. The second reason is that Yahya Kemal also was a bohemian and had an independent disposition like Hafız. For that reason, he wrote a poem about Hafız. Since Itri was a poet who understood Hafız and was a great composer, for his Neva Kar he chose one of his most touching gazels. This is why Itri and Yahya Kemal come together. Although in some sources it is stated that Hafız's divan contains 571 gazels, a copy that was printed in 1302 by the Ahter printing press, there are 579 gazels. According to this edition, the words of the Neva Kar are comprised of the first three couplets of the 485th gazel and the first couplet of the 90th gazel.

Itri who was in love with this gazel was able to bring out the meaning of every line in his music. Therefore, Itri is not only the leader of the composers but the leader of poetic composers.

OTTOMAN SOUNDS

Selim III

1760 - 1808

Magnificent
Ottoman Composers

A Progressive Sultan and His Time

T

he eighteenth century is an Islahat (reordering and modernization) period in which sultans such as Ahmet III, Mahmut I and Abdulhamid I lived. Mustafa III, Selim III's father, was a Sultan open to modernization who brought specialists from Europe.

The reign of Selim III, who even in his time as heir to the throne was of this inclination, is considered the most important step in Westernization before the Tanzimat. It is a period in which reforms in administration, agriculture and economy were targeted in view of European science and technology. Nizam-ı Cedid, "New Order," means the reforms that were made in military and political matters. These modernization efforts against all the difficult conditions of the period were very functional in modernization and change of Ottoman social organizations. In order to implement Nizam-ı Cedid, officially proclaimed on 24 February 1793, the Nizam-I Cedid Treasury and Finance Office were established and in addition to the Janissaries and Imperial Guard had started a new modern army giving modern infantry training on a farm in Levent. The artillery works and gunpowder mills were modernized, the shipyards were enlarged and the Mühendishane-i Berr-i Hümayun (an engineering school for educating artillery officers) was established. In addition to the building of barracks in Selimye and Levent, application of European methods to city life and art works had started during this period. An Austrian gardener, J. Ensle was brought to give a European look to the royal palace gardens. Architects and artists like Melling and Castellan, were invited. A dance teacher and several musicians were brought from France. The royal meşkhane was reorganized and the musicians were given monthly stipends.

This painting Selim III. is the most reknown (An oilpainting made by Konstantin Kapıbağlı on 1804 in Topkapı Palace Museum).

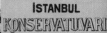

İSTANBUL
KONSERVATUVARI
NEŞRİYATI

Türk Musikisinin Klasikleri

№ 161

ÜÇÜNCÜ SELİM

SUZİDİLÂRA MAKAMINDA
AĞIR ve YÜRÜK SEMAİLER

KONSERVATUVARDAKİ İLMİ HEY'ET TARAFINDAN
TETKİK ve KABUL EDİLMİŞTİR.
HER HAKKI MAHFUZDUR

FİATI 5 KURUŞ

𝕴f one looks at this Europeanization from a wider perspective, it can be seen that the ascendance of Selim III to the throne on 8 April 1789 an event which occupies a significant place in human history, the French Revolution, 14 July 1789 wasn't a mere coincidence. The effects of this revolution which started with the occupation of the Bastille by the Parisians was naturally felt during Selim III's reign during which time the Ottomans were getting weaker both militarily and politically, the state was being reorganized and several contacts were being made with the West. (When he was heir to the throne, Selim III had had correspondence with Louis XVI.) During this period which was spent in wars, or preparation for wars, against Russia and Austria, technological improvements were necessary and steps had to be taken to prevent the collapse of the state starting with the economy, all of which was realized by Selim III. Under war conditions, product shortages, local rebellions against heavy taxes, fires and epidemics were rampant in Istanbul. The Sultan felt that extraordinary measures had to be taken and this could be done through Nizam-ı Cedid, which meant the application of European standards to the armed forces.

Several historians have pointed to the fact that the Sultan was inexperienced, highly emotional, selected the wrong people and generally made mistakes in his administration. People's problems were ignored but his innovations were also met with resistance by the reactionary religious clergy, Janissaries and illiterate people. These reforms, which were in essence the beginning of the slow disappearance of Ottoman independence, caused animosity. Along with this, the Sultan further alienated the people by spending his time on moonlight cruises, in mansions and houses on the Bosphorus, and this was interpreted as the "European way of doing things that were deemed to be a part of the New Order" (Mustafa Nuri Pasha, Netayicü'l - Vukuat).

The question of how Selim III was seen by his contemporaries and what his image in Europe was can be answered by referring to the European archives.

The most detailed study of this period that has been the subject of much research abroad, belongs to the American historian, Stanford Shaw. Shaw also considers Selim as a modernist but his reforms did not reach a level which could have incorporated them into the social and political reforms of the West. The generally accepted characterization of this period as a "window opening to the West" continues to be the case until today.

Selimiye Mosque in
İstanbul, Üsküdar.

The "Ney" against the sword

He was the 28th Ottoman Sultan born at Topkapı Palace on 24 December 1761 and died on 28 July 1808. His reign lasted from 7 April 1789 to 29 May 1807. He is the son of Sultan Mustafa III and Mihrişah Valide Sultan. He ascended the throne replacing his uncle, Abdülhamit I. Selim III whose birth was celebrated for seven days and nights with festivities and whose education started at an early age, lost his father at the age of 13 and during the reign of Abdülhamit I, who replaced his father, he spent the next 15 years in the Golden Cage. This was a period in which he spent his time with music and poetry, tried to follow world events and in order to learn more about military and industrial developments in Europe, corresponded with the French ambassador to Istanbul and Louis XVI. Selim III, who ascended the throne upon the death of his uncle, started implementing the ideas that had taken shape in his mind with regard to actions to be taken in view of the developments in the West. While grappling with foreign problems he was also trying to neutralize the opposition to the new order, particularly shown by the Janissaries, and stem the rioting in Istanbul (for example, prohibition of alcohol and general degeneration were some of the problems that the new sultan had to face). The changes in Europe's social life that were a consequence of the French Revolution which took place during this same period, the tense relations with Russia and other European countries made urgent the restructuring of the armed forces. The edicts issued by the Sultan to put under control luxurious living in view of the disintegration of the economy were met with resistance by the bureaucracy and at the same time continual bad news coming from the borders where territory was being lost. Fires, robberies, epidemics; famine, increase in corruption, the difficulty of maintaining order had the people depressed, and Napoleon's occupation of Egypt in 1798 made conditions even

Selim III. with his father, Mustafa II.

Selim III.'s helmet.

worse. The Sultan's spending his time with music at the Aynalıkavak Palace and occupying himself with only construction projects met with protests and during this period, war was officially declared against France. Internal strife was temporarily halted after this war that lasted until 1801, but the mutiny of the conservative circles and Janissaries continued to rumble against the application of the New Order. In 1806 the New Order (Nizam-ı Cedid) units proceeding toward Thrace were met with resistance (Edirne Incident) and rumors were rampant that Selim III would be dethroned. The year 1807 began with the loss of Belgrade, declaration of war against Russia, Serbian insurrection, and the

A painting of the war Akka.

occupation of Hicaz. To all these negative developments were added the anchoring of the British fleet in front of Yeşilköy and the rumors that Istanbul would be bombarded made the situation very tense. These general developments led to the Kabakcı Mustafa Rebellion on 25 May 1807 and resulted in the dethronement of Selim III on the 29th of May.

After this, Selim III withdrew to his quarters and spent his time reading the Koran and playing the ney unaware that Alemdar Mustafa Pasha who was intending to put him back on the throne, was killed by men sent by Mustafa IV. It is rumored that Selim III tried to defend himself with his ney against the blows of daggers and swords. The murdered Sultan was buried in the mausoleum of his father in Laleli with a great state funeral.

Selim III as a Musician

Selim III is an important musician who effectuated almost a turning point in the cultural and musical history of the Turkish people. In addition to his playing the tanbur, the ney and singing, his most important characteristic is his being a composer. Furthermore, due to his being absorbed in the arts from the time of his princehood, he gave great support to the arts and education. Very important works were done during his reign and many high level musicians flourished.

As was mentioned earlier, this period was open to modernism and change in the traditional direction of the Ottomans. This also affected the musical field and resulted in new composition forms, usage of melody and possibly related to this involved different ways of interpreting the performance of their works. It can be said that this general change in style was in a way a time of comparing itself with Western music, to reevaluate its own worth and to some extent compete with it.

Selim III who for the first time had Western music performed in the Topkapı Palace and watched an opera performed by a foreign group in 1797 also encouraged the local musician to organize a palace music school and put them on monthly stipends. The man who with the help of some French officers founded the first Drum and Bugle Corps to accompany

Muhayyer Sümbül Semâi
Üçüncü Selim

the New Order units (first step in the Western marching band) is the same man who at the same time encouraged local musicians such as Hamparsum and Abdülbaki Nasır Dede to codify classical Turkish music – in other words, Selim III.

The Sultan also made a special effort to combine makams and according to various sources succeeded in creating 14 to 15 of such composite makams. Some of these are: suzidilara, rast-i ceded, hicazeyn, şevk-i dil, arazbar buselik, neva kürdi, gerdaniye kürdi, hüseyni zemzeme...

It is known that his singing teacher was Müezzinbaşı Kırımlı Ahmet Kamil Efendi and his tanbur teacher was Ortaköylü Tanburı Hoca İsak Efendi. I. Hakkı Uzunçarşılı lists along with the salaries they received, starting with important musicians such as Vardakosta Ahmed Ağa, Tanburi Eyüp Ağa, and Kemani Hızır Ağa. Other names are Kemani Miron, tanbur teachers Hüseyin, Osman and Eyüp, singer Derviş İsmail (Dede Efendi), Santuri Huseyin Ağa...Also great composers who have composed some of the most important works of Turkish classical music such as Abdülhalim Ağa, Sadullah Ağa, Tanburi Emin Ağa, Numan Ağa, Kömürcuzade Hafız Mehmet Efendi, Küçük Mehmed Ağa lived during this period.

Zâvil makaminda Yürük semâi Üçüncü Selimin

Selim III

The soldiers of Nizam-ı Cedid, salute Selim III. in the first ceremony.

This period is considered a school in various sources due to musicians and developments. Some events that are relayed about that period describe its atmosphere. For example, Ahmet Rasim Bey in the third volume of his history, states that Selim III very much appreciated criticisms and discussions about his works. He would get opinions of

The Humbaracılar Barracks, built for the Humbaracı soldiers, in Sütlüce, in 1792.

the other musicians and when they only praised his work, he would get angry. Musicians were uneasy during the performance of a song with the words "I shout with the remembrance of the rose tuft of your hair," in the Şevkutarab makam when they discovered that there was something missing in the mode in the background portion of the song in the zencir tempo. But they had difficulty in pointing this out and they were very disturbed when during the performance there was a stoppage at this point. Finally, Vardakosta Ahmed Ağa had the courage to point this out, upon which Selim III stated that he was aware of the situation but could not find any other way to tie the melodies together; he knew this was contrary to tempo and rules and was very glad that this was pointed out to him, praised him and gave him gifts.

It was again Selim III who invited Hammami-zade İsmail to the palace. İsmail had become famous by composing a song in the muselik makam during the second year of his religious ordeal at the Yenikapı Mevlevi Lodge and continued to support him until he died.

It is written in the Esrar Dede book that Hafız Şeyda while he was serving as the head drummer in the Mevlevi was sent on the holy pilgrimage by Selim III.

His works, the mirror of a romantic personality

Selim III, who composed in many different forms is a genius according to many recent sources headed by Rauf Yekta Bey. He has a wide spectrum of works including religious works, instrumental works and many others, the majority of which are in higher forms (kar, beste, semai). The number of his works surviving to this day varies according to different sources but 103 are listed in the Musical Encyclopedia.

The most famous are: suzidilâra peşrev, beste and semaîs; zavil yürük semaî; şehnaz, muhayyer sünbüle, şevkefzâ, hüzzam, buselik, acemaşiran makamsda which are classical music in simple Turkish.

Selim III: The Poet: İlhami

As is well known, in the tradition of divan poetry poets used noms de plume and many times their real names were forgotten. Sometimes, utilizing the literal meaning of the nom de plume, they wrote poems making use of the meaning of their pseudonym. İlhami was the nom de plume used by Selim III. His father, Mustafa III, wrote poems under the name, Ikbali. The poems of other sultans and poets are not collected in any particular form.

The collection of poems written by the same poet in different forms such as kaside, gazel, murabba, is called a "Divan" and in order to be accepted as a poet, one had to have a Divan. Divans of some poets were organized posthumously by others. Selim III or "İlhami" has a Divan of some 200 pages. According to some historians, these poems reflect a man of high sensitivity and as a result, indecisiveness. Considering the conditions in which he grew up, his constant struggle to survive in an atmosphere in which the grabbing and maintaining of power was the most important thing, it is understandable the psychology that turned him to the pursuit of music and poetry.

The immense human dimension and his self criticism reflected in his poems is very intriguing. This can be seen in the following line: A famous poet of that period and a Mevlevi elder, Dervish Şeyh Galib, had a great influence on Selim and he maintained a very close relationship until his death. This affinity in the concept of art is evident in the structure of his poems. Additionally, a characteristic that is common to many Divan poets can also be found in him. He also wrote poems reflecting the tastes of the common people in simple Turkish and using syllabic meter. Quite a few of these became songs.

Even if Selim III had not been a musician, he was a Sultan who would take an important place in Ottoman art from a literary standpoint and also was a man who gave great support and was a patron of the arts.

Selim III. used the pseudonym "İlhami" for his poems; a painting from his İlhamî Divân.

"Selim-i Sâlis, Musician"

auf Yekta Bey, in the 16th issue of "Yeni Mecumua" (New Magazine) published on 25 October 1915, wrote an article, "Selim-i Sâlis, Mûsıkîşinas" (Selim III, Musician) in which he recounted his musical side, the music atmosphere during this period, his patronage of the arts by citing many examples and added the notes of his "buselik" song starting with the words, "Bir pür-cefâ hoş dilberdir". "She is full of struggle and a pleasant beauty." Rauf Yekta Bey starts his article by stating that even though the Selim III period was very rich in musical terms, history books do not contain any reference to the atmosphere that was conducive to the development of music. Only the Ata history made a perfunctory reference to the

Şeyh Galib.

developments in musicology and that only in conjunction with modernization attempts in science and technology. Also, the names of master musicians are listed which number a great deal more than any other period.

Rauf Yekta Bey continues to state that interest in music did not stop after Selim III; musicians still were held in esteem and as a result the accumulation of knowledge continued to be disseminated by word of mouth and he himself learned from the masters.

The Galata Dervish Lodge

Dervish lodges, which have had a very significant influence on Istanbul's cultural life, were five in number with the most important one being the Galata Dervish Lodge. This lodge was built during the reign of Bayezid II in 1491, and served as a focal point of political and social events for hundreds of years. It was a center for arts and culture toward the end of its existence and was closed in 1925. It now serves as a Museum of Divan Literature.

It is known that, especially under the tutelage of its last two sheikhhs, Dede Ataullah and Dede Ahmed Celaleddin, this lodge attracted the attention of a great many intellectuals, was a center where philosophical and sociological discussions were held and was a cultural center where musical theory was expanded. It is one of the most important attributes of the Galata Dervish Lodge that the musicology of our times was developed there and important theoreticians such as Rauf Yekta Bey

and Dr. Suphi Ezgi frequented the place. One of the names that makes this Dervish Lodge very special is Şeyh Galib who is one of the giants of Divan literature. During the time that he was the head of the lodge, he made reforms parallel to Westernization efforts. A good example of this is the inclusion of the piano to the musical ensemble in the performance of Sufi music. This effort was very appropriate for the Selim III period.

Rauf Yekta Bey, in his article in the New Magazine, states that like many of the Ottoman sultans, Selim III was a member of the High Order of the Mevlevis, and that he showed great respect to Şeyh Galib Dede who was the head of the Kulekapısı (Galata)

Dervish Lodge and had the title of Poet Laureate and Peerless Sage. For these reasons Selim III would come to this lodge after attending the official Friday noon prayers together with the most important believers and dervishes of the day. Rauf Yekta Bey gives many examples of Selim III's special relation with Şeyh Galib and the lodge, adding the poems that Şeyh Galib wrote in honor of the repairworks done by Selim III to the lodge. He also mentions the two lines used as an inscription on the entrance of the lodge:

Did clean and renew this lodge, Sultan Selim III in the year 1206 (This corresponds to the year 1791.).

The fact that Selim III signed the book of the dervishes as Selim Dede is an example of his respect to this place and his humbleness.

There is some thought that this dervish lodge which had another major repair job during the reign of Mahmut II was a bit politicized, was used against the Janissary Bektashi group and that this policy continued during the period of Abdülmecid. The buildings of the Galata Dervish Lodge that are seen today are the buildings that were repaired in 1835.

Tanburi İsak

Tanburi İsak (his real name is Fresko Romano, 1745 – 1814), who was the tanbur teacher of Selim III, is one of the most important composers of Turkish classical music. This musician of Jewish origin who had been educated in the Palace School received a salary as a tanbur teacher and continually participated in musical performances in the presence of his student, the Sultan. There is a very famous anecdote that when Tanburi İsak came to the presence of Selim III, the Sultan would respectfully stand up and present him with a tanbur filled with gold pieces in appreciation of a peşrev (prelude) that he had composed. In his book, Life in Istanbul During the 13th century (Hicri calendar), Ministry of Fisheries Ali Riza Bey, relates another story. The event is like this: Selim III used to have the küme faslı at the Serdab Pavilion at Topkapı Palace. One evening when the performance of this fasıl was ordered, one of the most important members of this fasıl group, Tanburi İsak couldn't be found so they started the performance without him. A while later, İsak arrived but the Head Eunuch, since the fasıl had started, would not let him enter. İsak insisted. The argument heated up and was overheard by the Sultan. He immediately asked İsak to come and join them and the Head Eunuch, who had no special qualities, was chastised for not being respectful to an artist. This again proved how appreciate of art the Sultan was.

OTTOMAN SOUNDS

Hammâmî-zâde
İsmail

Dede
Efendi

Magnificent
Ottoman Composers

İSTANBUL
BELEDİYE
MECMUASI

HAMMAMI ZADE
İSMAİL DEDE
KONSERİ MÜNASEBETİLE

İLÂVE SAYI

7.10.1941

Hammâmî-zâde Ismâil Dede Efendi

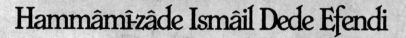

Dede Efendi whose name has become almost synonymous with Turkish music, lived at a time of the Ottoman Empire under Selim III, Mustafa IV, Mahmut II and Abdülmecit Han. This was a period of which old cultural traditions and institutions lived but were also being opened up to Western influences. Therefore, it is possible to trace the political and social developments through his understanding and art, which is reflected in his music. Also he attended the Yenikapı Dervish Lodge starting at a young age where he went through his "çile" (Ordeal) and obtained the rank of "Dede" in this order. This experience influenced his musical taste and his outlook on life and is another important factor in his sensitivity and style of production. His relationship with the palace and the dervish lodge certainly influenced his music. But he also took special care to be close to the people and the musical texts and forms that he used endeared him to the people thereby making him popular in various segments of society. In short, Dede Efendi takes his position at the center of the relationship between music and the people.

From a wider perspective, this all-encompassing position of Dede Efendi has a great meaning in our past culture that has been verbally past down to the present.

Mustafa IV.
(1779-1808).

Mahmut II.
(1785-1839).

Abdülmecid
(1823-1861).

Selim III.
(1761-1808).

A productive reformist

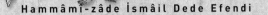

İsmail, who would take his place in musical literature as Dede Efendi, was born 9 January 1778 in a house near Şehzadebaşı. İsmail, at the age of 7, started his schooling at the "Çamaşırcı School which was next to the Hekimoğlu Ali Pasha Mosque and graduated from there. While attending this school, he caught the attention of the Anatolian Treasurer, Uncu-zade Seyyid Mehmed Efendi, who had his mansion next to the school and who was an important music master of that age. Uncuzade, who had one of his sons attending the same school, noticed and appreciated the beauty of İsmail's voice and his ability. İsmail was then serving as the head hymn-singer of the school. Mehmet Efendi put him among his special students and they together made music. When İsmail was 14, this man who saw him as his own son and protected him, wanting to guarantee his future had him appointed as an apprentice to the Head Accounting Office. İsmail, while working at this job, continued to go to the Yenikapı Dervish Lodge twice a week and took music lessons from the Şeyh Ali Nutki Dede Efendi and thus progressed considerably in the perfection of his art.

İsmail, who attended the lodge in order to learn music became enamored with his sheyk and the Mevlevi sect and in 1797 wanted to completely dedicate himself to the lodge and go through the Ordeal. He forced them to accept the situation even though his family and his teacher tried to dissuade him. During this period of the Ordeal, he studied the whirling and participated in whirling ceremonies and wore the special skirt. These are all mentioned in Şeyh Ali Kutki Dede's private writings. İsmail, who lost his father shortly thereafter, despite the protestations of his mother, sold the hamam and with the proceeds organized many ceremonies at the Lodge. In the second year of his Ordeal he composed a song in the buselik makam the words of which belong to Keçecizade İzzet

Molla and it went like this: "In your hair is my black fortune." This song became very popular among the people and in the musical circles. The reputation of this song finally reached the palace and was performed in the presence of Selim III. This opened the gates of the palace for him. Praised by the Sultan and rewarded by him, he continued to compose songs and his fame spread. In 1799 he completed his Ordeal, and his room in the Lodge was frequented by many music lovers.

His beautiful works that spread through the efforts of his apprentices at the Lodge makes the name of İsmail Dede better known. This fame caused Selim III, who himself was a composer, to want Dede Efendi to come to the palace on a continual basis. He was appointed as a singer in the fasıls performed in the palace, then became the Gentleman-in-Waiting of the Sultan; later being appointed the Head Muezzin (the one who calls the faithful to prayer).

It is rumored that the reason why he completed his Ordeal in less than 1001 days was the fact that Sultan Selim III wanted him at the palace. After he was at the palace, he could only go to the Lodge on the days of religious ceremonies.

Hammâmî-zâde İsmâil Dede Efendi

It is stated that Dede, who was only 22 years old at that time, could not have been a Gentleman-in-Waiting of the sovereign and the head muezzin, and according to the anecdotes of the Palace School: "This could have been possible at the time of Mahmut II."

The importance that is attached to music in the Ottoman palace tradition can be understood by the special place that music teaching was given in the Palace School. This was a school that took young boys and gave them special training in the fine arts and general culture.

Music is in a way part and parcel of the reign of this sultanate and its way of life. This is proven by the fact that many of the Ottoman sultans and statesmen were themselves musicians who took part in our history as performers or composers. Additionally there always were special musical groups at the palace at all times. It is important that Dede Efendi was at the center of the Ottoman capital's musical life for a long time that started with Selim III, continued with the reign of Mahmut II and Abdülmecit, apart from short interruptions. He used the opportunity of influencing the artistic understanding of this period through his compositions, performances and musical taste combining it with the humility and non-elitist approach that came from his being a dervish.

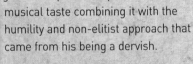

(It is known that Dede Efendi, who did not interrupt his relations with the Dervish Lodge also learned to play the ney from Nasır Seyyid Abdülbaki Dede who was the brother of Ali Nutki Dede.) Dede Efendi at the beginning of 1802 married a lady from the palace, left his cell at the lodge and moved to a house in the Akbıyık section and toward the end of that year a son by the name of Salih was born.

Yenikapı Mevlevihanesi.

The death in 1804 of Ali Nutki Dede who was his beloved sheikh and master grieved Dede Efendi very much. Not long after this loss, his son Salih died at the age of 3 grieving Dede Efendi further.

On top of all these sorrowful events, 3 years later in 1808, he lost his mother Rukiye Hanım, and his second son, Mustafa, also died. Dede Efendi entered in which he did not have the will to make any music.

During this time there were many disturbances in various parts of the Empire. Sultan Selim III was dethroned and later killed, which caused a sense of sorrow throughout the Empire. In the meantime, he left his job as Head Muezzin and moved from the palace. A period started in which he dedicated himself to dervishhood and to life at the Lodge and to composing music. While there were a total of 14 Mevlevi ayins composed by the beginning of the 19th century, through Dede Efendi's efforts, the number reached 46 by the end of the century. Dede Efendi in 1823 composed two ayins, the first one in the sabah makam and the second in the neva makam and when they were performed in the lodge they caused quite a stir.

Hammâmî-zâde İsmâil Dede Efendi

Mahmut II was visiting the Yenikapı Dervish Lodge while the neva ayın was being performed to a large crowd. Remembering Dede, the Sultan ordered him to be taken to the palace again and appointed him as Gentleman-in-Waiting. His return to the palace was not well received by the other musicians and knowing his greatness in music, they were afraid of the competition. It is said that the Head Muezzin, Şakir Ağa who himself was a famous and important composer was jealous of Dede Efendi and wanted to belittle him in the presence of the Sultan. For that reason, Şakir Ağa created a new makam (ferahnak) and planned to perform songs that he composed in this makam and thereby intimidate Dede Efendi. In this struggle, Dede Efendi came out on top.

Dede Efendi later continued to compose in the grand form works such as: bestenigâr âyin, buselik faslı, sabâ-buselik âyin, hüzzam âyin. He also became the Head Muezzin and by composing religious hymns, he performed them with the muezzins.

Dede Efendi influenced many composers during his time and later taught the likes of Dellalzâde İsmail Efendi along with Eyyubî Mehmet Bey, Hacı Ârif Bey, Hâşim Bey, Mutafzâde Ahmed Efendi, Yağlıkçızâde Ahmed Efendi. The fact that his songs were performed extensively and had a widespread reputation and particulary through the efforts of his student Zekai Dede to reach modern

times, saved many of Dede Efendi's works from oblivion.

Dede Efendi, whose fame was spreading throughout the 31-year reign of Mahmut II who died in 1839, remained at the Palace during the reign of the young Sultan Abdülmecit I.

Abdülmecit I had training in Western music and was not very fond of the local music and thus songs that were simpler and with dubious artistic value, began to spread. This upset Dede Efendi. Dede Efendi who was open to new things and composed many songs in the semai usul like Kar-ı Nev which means "New Work," in the end said, "The game is over," and decided to go on pilgrimage. In 1846, together with Zeki Mehmet Ağa, Dellalzade and Mutafzade, he went on pilgrimage.

He caught cholera there which was widespread and on the morning of the bayram, he died at Mina. Ibnülemin Mahmut Kemal Bey relates by referring to Bolahenk Nuri Bey that Dede Efendi died in the arms of Mutafzade Ahmet Efendi who was known as Dede's gramophone because he immediately memorized all his works. Dede Efendi's funeral was attended by many and he was buried at the foot of Hazreti Hatice.

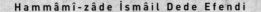

An art life rich with prizes

Dede Efendi is a composer of genius magnitude. He was very productive and throughout his life was rewarded including a medallion covered with precious stones given to him by Mahmut II. It is known that he composed about 500 works, ranging from very artistic and grand forms to folk songs and köçekçe. According to information given by Yilmaz Öztuna, we have 288 of his works with notes (56 religious and 232 non-religious).

The Ferahfeza Kar (Kazr-ı Cennet) which Dede Efendi composed as a result of a request by Mahmut II was a work that Dede Efendi liked very much. The classical set he created out of his makam is one of the masterpieces of Turkish classical

A hand writing of İsmâil Dede Efendi.

repetoire. The Ferahfeza ayın that he composed at the request of Mahmut II who insisted on attending the first performance at the Yenikapı Mevlevi Lodge even though he was sick is also very artistic. However, it is said that he thought this work did not have enough spirit in it since it was composed at the instigation of the Sultan and not at the request and wish of his Şeyhs.

The one who created and used the araban-kürdî, hicaz puselik, sabâ-puselik, nev'eser and sultaniyegâh makams for the first time was Dede Efendi. Of the seven ayins that he composed, one has been lost. His other religious works are: 1 savt, 4 tevşih, 3 durak, and 37 ilâhîdir. He also has four instrumental works and 232 secular works.

In addition to his works like the yürük semai in the hicaz makam starting with the words, "Once again the joy of love made my heart and soul mad" and "Once again the boat-shaped handle of my heart is broken," a yürük semai in the mahur makam which are grand and perfect, his simple and much loved songs like "A young rose has taken my heart" and "Oh, new form idol" are known and sung by everyone even today.

The house that Dede Efendi lived in toward the end of his life in the Akbıyık neighborhood of Cankuturan after being in ruins for years has now been restored and open to the public as the Dede Efendi House (by the Society for the Preservation of Historical Turkish Homes):

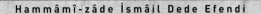

Dede Efendi's House

The last house in which Dede Efendi lived in the Akbıyık section of Istanbul has been turned into a cultural center. Rauf Yekta Bey, after seeing it abandoned in 1920 wrote the following in his biography. This passage from the biography is simplified below: "In 1258 (1840) Dede Efendi heard of a mansion that was available near Ahırkapı and since he was tired of living in rented homes and he was sure of the Sultan's generosity toward him, put in a request for this house to be presented to him. Sultan Abdülmecit immediately accepted the request and ordered that the rent for the mansion be paid to the foundation from the Treasury and that the place should be presented to Dede Efendi.

"Since I had heard that this mansion was still in existence, I made a special trip and found this building. Opposite the mosque, there is a fountain and on the other side of the mosque is the Akbıyık hamam. Exactly facing this mosque and next to the fountain one can see a red building. This was the selamlık part of the house. The harem section behind had already fallen down and the land is now being used by the military as a depot. Since the door was open, I entered and if I had seen anyone there I would have asked for permission to enter. Apparently, a refugee was

settled there. I was sorry to see the condition of the mansion   Looking at the stairs that started at the entrance, I could imagine seeing Eyyubi Mehmet Bey and his student, Hafız Zekai Efendi, climbing these stairs. Realizing that what was left of the building would be gone in a few years, I sadly left the place.

"While reading the biographies of the important composers in the West, I noticed how the municipalities took care of the homes where they were born, lived and died from the pictures that were published.

"I think that Dede Efendi's place in Turkish music history is not any less than the place that these Western musicians have in the history of their own country. Therefore, wouldn't it be better if this mansion was taken over by the municipality, restored to its original position and taken care of in a proper way and on the anniversary of Dede Efendi's death a ceremony be held there. This would show the gratitude of the people for the man and also motivate young people who would want to be musicians themselves.

"In the West, they put up statues of people famous in their professions. This is a beautiful tradition that doesn't exist in our country but I am sure will in due time. While waiting for that time to come, at least we can wish that we appreciate the value of people like Dede Efendi."

The Visit of Mahmut II to the Dervish Lodge

Thanks to the support and prizes that he received from Mahmut II, Dede Efendi composed many songs and dedicated quite a few of them to the Sultan. A good example of this is the visit of Mahmut II even though he was sick to the dervish lodge for the first performance of the Ferahfeza ayin. This event is written about extensively in his book entitled "Masters of Melody." In the third section entitled "Dede Efendi," Rauf Yekta Bey relates the following story (Istanbul 1340 – (1924) p. 163); in simplified form: "Mahmut II after hearing the performance of the Ferahfeza fasıl at the Serdab Palace, liked this very much – so much so that during performances in his presence, he requested that this fasıl be performed.

The mevlevis made good use of this fact of the Sultan's liking this makam. Mahmut II who had sympathy and good will toward the mevlevi sect frequently went to the Beşiktaş Dervish Lodge on Wednesdays and attended the ayins.

One Wednesday after the whirling ceremony, the Sultan called Dede and told him: 'My Dede, you know how much I like Ferahfeza, I would be very happy if you were to compose an ayın in this makam.' Upon this royal directive, Dede Efendi composed a very colorful and joyful ayin and a peşrev. We had already mentioned that Dede was a master ney player. In this connection, let's record that in

The Dedegân room of Mevlevîhâne of Yenikapı.

addition to the perşrev that he composed for the Ferahfeza ayin, he also composed peşrevs for the Bestenigar and Sabapuselik ayins. These peşrevs show how masterful Dede Efendi was in composing instrumental music. At the end of the year 1254 (1838), Mahmut II was somewhat depressed as his sickness was continuing. Since the Ferahfeza ayin was composed upon the request of the Sultan, it was rehearsed by the muezzins of the lodge most of whom were Dede's students. It was decided that this masterpiece would be performed on the 18th of Muharrem 1255 (1839) which was a Wednesday, at the Beşiktaş Dervish Lodge with a great deal of pomp and the Sultan was duly informed. The day of the ayin, the Beşiktaş lodge filled with numerous sheikhs, dervishes, friends and musicians

As the people were waiting for the arrival of the Sultan, an aide to the Sultan came to the lodge and informed them that his royal highness was not feeling well and therefore it was doubtful that he would be attending the mukabele but the Ferahfeza ayin was to be performed at the wish of the Sultan. This news naturally disappointed the crowd but they made their preparations and they went to the semahane (meeting rooms). They had just started to perform the blessing when contrary to what was expected, the Sultan appeared at the lodge. This acted as an incentive and the Ferahfeza ayin was performed with great gusto. After the ceremony, the Sultan called Dede Efendi and said 'I was very sick – I wasn't going to come. I made a special effort to come and I am glad I did. The ayin acted as an elixir of life to me – Thank God, I am almost well...' Thus complimenting him extensively, as a thanks for the royal healing, the Sultan gave gifts to all the dervishes starting with the sheikh of the lodge."

Yenikapı Mevlevîhânesi.

Hoca Mehmed

Zekâi
Dede

1825 - 1897

Magnificent
Ottoman Composers

رؤف يكتا

أساتيذ الحان

شرق وغرب مشاهير موسيقى شناسانك تراجم احوالى ايله
آغازئفيسه ومؤلفات برگزيدهلرى حقنده معلومات مكملهيى
حاوى بر اثردركه اجزاسى بيدربى نشر ايدلهجكدر

برنجى جزء : خواجه زكائى دده افندى

معارف نظارت جليلهسنك فى ١١ صفر
سنه ١٣١٨ تاريخ و ١١١ نومرولى
رخصتنامهسيله طبع اولنمشدر

استانبول
(محمود بك) مطبعهمى — باب عالى جوارنده ابوالسعود جادهسنده نومرو ٧٢
١٣١٨

Hoca Mehmed Zekâi Dede

ekâi Dede is unanimously described as "the last grand classic, the last grand composer." In a more analytical form, he is referred to as the last of Dede Efendi's classical school. That he lived during a time when the Tanzimat and Westernization played havoc with the Ottoman cultural, social and political norms - the last three-quarters of the 19th century – makes this description even more important. During a period when music forms changed, became lighter and - especially the şarkı (song) - spread and instead of the old makams and usuls, livelier and faster rhthyms were being used, Zekai Dede stands alone as a man still dedicated to the old understanding of music.

The works that he composed with this understanding, his way of life and the students that he educated puts him aside as a man who has withstood time. The title given to Zekai Dede today as the last representative of the classical tradition in addition to being a technical reality, gives him his due.

When compared to Hacı Arif Bey, who was born in the same neighborhood and who was his student later on, the difference in their musical style is quite apparent and this makes his conscientious choice for classical music more important.

The founder of modern musicology

e was born at the beginning of 1825 in a house next to the Cedid Ali Paşa Mescidi. His father, Hafız Süleyman Hikmeti Efendi, was the imam of the neighborhood (later on both Zekai Efendi and his son Ahmet Efendi also served as imams at the same mescid). He started to learn the Koran and calligraphy from his father and uncle and attended the Lalizade Primary School. After finishing this school, he completed his memorization of the Koran, received a diploma in calligraphy, and took high school lessons from the then-famous sage, Balçıklı Hoca Ali Efendi.

It should be pointed out that the short biography written in the early 1900s by Rauf Yekta Bey, who was a student of Zekai Dede toward the

end of his life, is a source of important information about this composer. Additionally, like Rauf Yekta Bey, Dr. Suphi Ezgi who also was a student of Zekai Dede was instrumental in recording compositions that he learned from him. From a wider perspective, the students of Zekai Dede who in turn was one of the best students of Dede Efendi, are among the founders of modern Turkish musicology. This continuity is very important for modern-day Turkish music.

Rauf Yekta Bey during a rehearsal with Zekai Dede at the Şah Sultan Dervish Lodge heard Zekai Dede say that he had composed an ayin in the Süzidil makam but it had never been performed. Upon the insistence of all present, they started practicing this ayin. It was performed at the Bahariye Dervish Lodge on a Wednesday the 17th of Şaban, 1309 under the direction of Zekai Dede and his students. Rauf Yekta Bey said he could never forget how pleased Zekai Dede was and he profusely thanked every one of them.

In the biography written by Rauf Yekta Bey there are many incidents like these and they are written in a very sentimental and free-flowing manner. Zekai Efendi progressed considerably as a result of lessons that he took from Eyyubi Mehmed Bey, and in the meantime learned some new calligraphy forms from the famous calligrapher and musician, Kazasker Mustafa İzzet Efendi. Then a very fortuitous meeting took place. In 1844 when he was 20, he had been going to Hammami-zade İsmail Dede Efendi for about a year and learning from him about the intricacies of music, and in 1845 he met the Egyptian prince Mustafa Fazıl Bey (later Vezir Mustafa Fazıl Pasha) and went to Cairo as his special musician.

Hoca Mehmed Zekâi Dede

He came back to Istanbul - in the meantime, Dede Efendi died during his pilgrimage in 1846. After a short stay, he went back to Egypt and lived there for another 6 years and upon the appointment of Mustafa Fazıl Pasha as a vezir and cabinet member he returned to Istanbul permanently. This music-loving statesman supported, encouraged and provided a comfortable life for Zekai Dede for a period of 30 years. For example, Zekai Dede composed the Süzidil ayin mentioned earlier for Mustafa Fazıl Pasha in one night. When he listened to the performance of the ayin, the Pasha could not keep the tears from flowing and showed his appreciation to the master composer by giving him a bag of gold coins. This was relayed by his son Ahmet Efendi.

Zekai Efendi did not have any relations with a dervish lodge until 1868 when he started attending the Yenikapı Dervish Lodge. Here the composer would perform the ayin twice a week. Iin 1885 upon the recommendation of his student Hüseyin Fahreddin Dede, sheikh of the Bahriye Dervish Lodge, Zekai Dede was appointed head drummer at the lodge and some time late obtained the title of Dede even though he did not go through the customary Ordeal. He composed four mevlevi ayins – one after the other – at this lodge which he had entered as a 60-year-old mature composer. The makams that he chose for his ayins were different from the makams chosen by his teacher, Dede Efendi. Zekai Dede, who continued his position as head drummer for 13 years until his death, at the same was a teacher of music at the Darüşşafaka School. It is reported that he knew Western and Hamparsum notes but chose not to use them, played the ney and spoke both Arabic and Persian.

Suphi Ezgi, together with five or six of friends, became his student for two and a half years, starting when the master was 72 years old, at the Eyüb Şahsultan Tekkesi Hünkar Mahfili. Reporting that he would teach them for five or six hours, described his teacher thus: "He was 72 years old, he did not have a good voice but his singing was very strong. He would keep the beat and pronounce the sounds well." Zekai Dede taught many students, starting with his own son Hafız Ahmet Efendi and including Ahmed Avni Konuk, Hüseyin Fahreddin Dede, Muallim Kazım Uz, Ahmet Rasim Bey. His health started to deteriorate toward 1897, but he did not give up any of his duties. Rauf Yekta Bey, who was privy to this situation and was very sad about it, relayed that one day when he was returning from the Bahariye Dervish Lodge he ran into Tophaneli Sabri Bey who was one of Zekai Dede's best students and they shared their sorrow. He could not go to the music lessons the following week and learned of Zekai Dede's death from the Ikdam newspaper. He relays at length how saddened he was and how he went and found the grave and goes on to tell about his feelings.

Zekai Dede died on 24 November 1897 and is buried near the Eyüp Kaşgari Dervish Lodge.

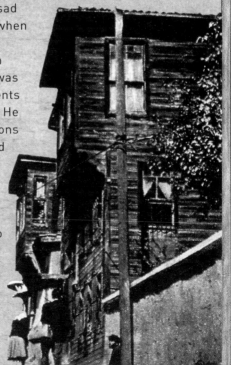

**House of Zekâi Dede
Eyüp Kurukavak st. 84.**

A didactic approach to melody

Müstear song at Zekâi Dede Efendi.

Zekai Dede after only one year of taking lessons from Eyyubi Mehmet Bey was able to compose some songs and ilahi. Hafız Ahmed Efendi who gives the above information, says the following about his music: although his musical style is similar to Dede Efendi's and Mehmet Bey's, the late Zekai Efendi, had added some specialties to them; therefore, his works have a different color and content. He is the last of the musicians from the Dede Efendi School. Aside from the 5 ayins that he composed, the number of ilahis, songs and şuulat (ilahis with words in Arabic) is over 400. He also has about 100 murabba, kar, nakş semai in the grand form each of which is more valuable than the other; it is not possible to choose one over the other.

His service to religious music has been immense. His works are unique examples of Turkish music. Every line has a different sweetness to it.

Ahmed Efendi is the source for all this information about his works and is the main instrument for his father's compositions to reach our day. He published the Zekai Dede Works at the conservatory and took part in the group that prepared the Mevlevi Ayins which were published in a book. Only half of Zekai Dede's works have survived to the present.

In the Zekai Dede collections the number of secular works published by Dr. Suphi Ezgi and Hafız Ahmed Efendi is 117. When looking at his kar-ı natık, kar, beste, semai, which are all in the grand form and number about 40, one can see the totality of Zekai Dede's style. An ever-present didactism which is not dry, a prosody that is faultless and constructed carefully, a high musical taste are present in all his works from the ordinary to the grand. He has combined rhythm and melody with great taste and fineness. Rauf Yekta Bey states that in the last century (meaning the 19th) of all the musical masters, Zekai Dede is only second to Dede Efendi in important. He composed in almost every form. It is impossible to select any of his works over the others.

It is necessary to speak of the contribution of Zekai Dede to mevlevi music which has all the makings of classical music (the notes of 5 mevlevi ayins and 130 works of different forms have reached our day. His ayins are in the ısfahan, süz-i dil, maye, suznak and saba zemzeme makams). Saadettin Nüzhet Ergün wrote that among Turkish composers the one who composed the most religious works after Ali Şir ü Gani is Zekai Dede. "an important aspect of his works is the fact that they were sung by the people as well as the musicians." He described Zekai Dede's works as being not brisk and lively, but masterful and solemn and affecting one's conscience.

We can see in his son's discussions of him that he was able to compose very quickly and in fact while looking at the words of a poem, he would compose the song in his mind so that it could immediately be performed. It is known that he combined the hicaz aşiran and bayati-büselik makams and composed works in these combined forms.

Zekai Dede also has school marches and war songs. The two marches that he composed "during the war that took place between the Turks and the Greeks" is among his collection. Zekai Dede who has a very special place with his works in the, süzidil makam and his works in the hicazkar, hisar buselik, bayati classical works are unforgettable works of Turkish music repertoire.

Musical Education at Darüşşafaka and Zekai Dede

It can be said the it was thanks to Zekai Dede's working at Darüşşafaka, first on a voluntary basis (1873) and later as a paid teacher (1876), that the continuity of Turkish classical music was preserved, taking root through the efforts of such a master. In a period when the Tanzimat caused Westernization and affected many forms of social life, it is important that the musical inclinations of Zekai Dede were chosen and through the students he educated, this tradition was able to be continued. This is a first in the teaching of Turkish classical music. Darüşşafaka is the first school at a high school level that taught Turkish music as a separate course.

A group from "Hey'et-i Hâzine-i Talimiye"

In a book published by the school in 1927, the following was said about its music education: "It is necessary to reserve a special place for Zekai Dede among the former music teachers. When music was not being taught in any other schools, to have Zekai Dede who was the greatest musician of his time, first as a volunteer in 1293 and later appointed by the Education Society as a paid teacher in 1300, and who continued to teach until his death in 1313 and whose place was then taken by his son Hafız Ahmed Efendi – the totality of their work shows that musical education at Darüşşafaka has been going on for over half a century and that these men trained many musicians. Zekai Dede's complete biography is in the first volume of Masters of Rhythm.

When new students came to Darüşşafaka they would be assembled and asked to recite a section of the Koran. Then those with good voices and musical ability would be trained in music. In other words, musical education at Darüşşafaka was not general but specific in the beginning. Among Darüşşafaka graduates, it is thanks to this musical education that one can find those who chose music teaching as a profession at other schools and who wrote books about music. Ahmet Rasim Bey, in addition to being a successful author, was also a musician who could compose his own music and who had learned his music from Zekai Dede at Darüşşafaka."

Zekâi Dede, in Dârüşşafaka's garden, with his students.

Bahariye Dervish Lodge

The Beşiktaş Dervish Lodge, third after the Galata and Yenikapı Dervish Lodges, was built in 1622 during the construction of the Çirağan Palace. It was taken down and moved first to Fındıklı, later to Maçka and finally in 1877 to a new building in Eyüp Bahariye. The presence of Hoca Zekai Dede, known as the last classical master at this lodge that continued operations until 1925 when all tekkes were closed down by the Republic, was very important. Zekai Dede was the head sheikh of this lodge and was the teacher of Şeyh Hüseyin Fahreddin Dede (1854-1911), a ney player and a composer. The musical ability and love of music of Fahreddin Dede made the Bahariye Dervish Lodge the most important musical center of the period in Istanbul. The most famous and important musicians of the time such as Yeniköylü Hasan Efendi, Neyzen Aziz Dede, Zekai Dede, Havız Şevki Bey, Tophaneli Sabri Bey, Müstantik Avni Bey and İsmail Hakkı Bey attended this lodge and performed not only religious music but also other forms of classical music such as: kar, bestei and semai. These meetings that took place twice a week made it possible for religious and non-religious music to be memorized, and written into notes, a practice which was becoming more and more common in those days. Rauf Yekta Bey and Dr. Suphi Ezgi, who are among the founders of Turkish musicology, also attended these meetings and were able to pass on the music.

This cultural function is apparent when one looks at the Yenikapı, Galata and Bahariye Dervish Lodges, and to some lesser extent at the Kasımpaşa and Üsküdar Lodges. These places provided shelter and food and religious teaching along with being centers of social and artistic activities. They were supported by the sultans who encouraged the building and repairs of these places and often visited them.

The Bahariye Lodge, which underwent major repairs in 1328 (1910) was open with a grand ceremony attended by Sultan Reşat (Mehmet V). In the book entitled "Daily Life in Istanbul" Ekrem Işın describes this opening by summarizing Hüseyin Fahreddin Dede's periodical "At 7:30 (according to Moslem, ala turka time), the guests entered the semahane and at 8:00 the royal boat of Sultan Reşat docked. The Sultan was met by a crowd including Şeyhülislam Musa Kazım Efendi (Chief Religious Official) and Şerif Haydar Bey, the Minister in charge of Foundations, and given incense by Fahreddin Dede. After this they went to the semahane and watched the ceremony. The ceremony started with the recital of the mevlud by Fahreddin Dede's brother-in-law, Şevki Efendi, the chief muezzin of the Teşfikiye Mosque, Hafız Şükrü Efendi and Tahsin Efendi, the speaker of the Galata Lodge. It was followed by a prayer recited by Hüsnü Efendi who was the sheikh of the Balaban Tekke. Then the na't-ı şerife was recited by Zekai Dede, the chief drummer of the Bahariye Dervish Lodge and finally the ısfahan ayin was performed. After the ayin, Mehmet Kutbeddin Efendi, chief sheikh of the Kocamustafapaşa Asitanesi , performed the Sünbüli devrani and the kıyam tevhidi to end the ceremony.

Sitting (left to right): Yenikapı Mevlevîhâne's Postnişîn Mehmed Celâleddin Dede, Bahâriye Mevlevîhâne's Postnişîn Hüseyin Fahreddin Dede, Galata Mevlevîhâne's Postnişîn Mehmed Ataullah Dede.

Zekai Dede's Death, Histories and Eulogies

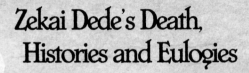

Rauf Yekta Bey speaks of the death of Zekai Dede that he learned from the press: "His death was announced with great sorrow by the Ottoman press. Also, famous poets and important people of the time wrote poems and chronograms and he gives three examples of these:

1.   "To the eloquent poems of saadetlu (official titles of generals), Hüseyin Haşım Bey Efendi, poet of sweet expressions, witty writer.

2.   "History of beautiful objects of saadetlu İsmet Bey Efendi, the Chief Secretary of the Imperial Chancery and a graceful poet of virtue.

3.   "The distinguish history which is the sagacious handwork of saadetlu Edhem Bey Efendi, one of the famous writers of the century, and chief secretary of the accounting office at the Imperial arsenal."

The last line of one of those chronograms, written by İsmet Bey, is as follows: "Zekai Dede paused at the final meeting place." This corresponds to the Moslem calendar 1315 and is a nice way of stating the date of his death in musical terms. The last line of a chronogram by Edhem Bey makes a play on words in the suzidil makam which Zekai Dede used extremely well in the makam in which he composed the first mevlevi ayin.

The students of Daru'l-Elhan, the famous compesers of Turkish Music, the teachers and the singers, on 1926.

Zekai-zade Ahmed Efendi (Irsoy)

*T*t is necessary to make a section for the man who was known simply as Hafız Ahmed Efendi but whose real name was Ahmet İlhami. He not only was the son of Zekai Dede and his musical heir apparent, but also occupied the role that was important for our modern day music. He carried the mantle of being the son of a most respected musician like Zekai Dede in a modest way. Hafız Ahmed Efendi was born in the Eyüp Cedid Ali Pasha neighborhood. He finished the Lalizade Primary School in Eyüp and became a hafız after taking lessons from his father and Hafız Osman Efendi. He also received a diploma from Hafız Süleyman Efendi and the imam of Eyüp Mosque, Hoca Raik Efendi, after taking lessons from them in Arabic, the Koran and Islamic theory. He entered the Mevlevi sect at a very young age. He learned playing the ney and Persian from the Hüseyin Fahreddin Dede, sheikh of the Bahariye Dervish Lodge. In 1885 he was appointed head drummer of this Dervish Lodge and after the death of his father, became the permanent head drummer. He also was the head drummer at the Yenikapı Dervish Lodge and he continued in these positions until 1925 when all religious lodges were closed down.

Hafız Ahmed Efendi, who learned calligraphy from his father and had many religious and non-religious meşks with him, became the imam of Şehzade Seyfeddin Efendi, the son of Sultan Abdülaziz and later chief mevlidhan of Sultan Vahdettin.

He also was a music teacher in several schools, mainly Darüşşafaka and Darülelhan, until his death in 1943, and educated many students through private lessons. He is mentioned as one of the key personages in music of the transition from the Ottomans to the Republic. He made many contributions at the conservatory by working with musicians like Rauf Yekta Bey, Dr. Suphi Ezgi, Ali Rıfat Bey and Mes'ud Cemil.

It is known that he learned the Hamparsum notation system from his teacher, ney player Emin Efendi and the Western notation system from his friend Rauf Yekta

Bey, who also was a student of his father. Dr. Suphi Bey, who refers to him as his master, states that he had a good voice and his rendition was very delicate.

Recently there have been publications analyzing his place in our music (people like Sadun Aksüt, Cem Behar) and these point to the fact that he was a transmitter of the old to the new.

He was reluctant to bring forth his compositions in the classical manner and for that reason only 50 to 60 of his compositions out of the 300 he wrote have survived. He composed a yürük semai in the sultaniyegah makam and when he performed it in front of his father, was rewarded with a silver coin. When one considers that he also composed two ayins, one in the bayati-buselik and the other in the müstear makam, it is apparent that he was very meticulous and attached great importance to music. His respect for his father and the music he represented caused him not to bring himself to the forefront. When one looks at his compositions in beste, semai and şarkı which all have classical forms and the religious works numbering 40, one can see the strong technical master.

There is some information to the fact that some of compositions reportedly written by Dede Efendi (all of which had been forgotten) were actually composed by Hafız Ahmed Efendi in the Dede Efendi style and memorized as Dede's.

Ahmed Efendi, who had heart troubles for a long time died in 1943 and is buried next to his father at the Eyüp Kaşgari Dervish Lodge. It is reported that very few people attended his funeral.

From a Pleasant Voice

"He learned music from his father who was known as the repository of the secrets of music and therefore he had mastery over the content and context of music. He did the meşk of the ney with Hüseyin Fahrüddin Dede Efendi, sheikh of the Behariyye Dervish Lodge and the na't and the composition on the holy ascent with the head drummer of the Yenikapı Dervish Lodge Ahmed Dede. Upon the death of his father, he was appointed as the music teacher at Darüşşafaka and also as head drummer at the Bahariye Dervish Lodge and upon the death of Ahmet Dede as the head drummer of the Yenikapı Dervish Lodge.

"He also served as the imam of the Cedid Ali Pasha Mosque and as a secretary at the mosque that is a continuation of the Hasib Efendi Lodge on Kalenderhane Street in Eyüp. He was a teacher at the Sultan Ahmet Middle School for Girls, at a religious high school and at Darülelhan.

"Martyred Prince Sa'id Halim Pasha having noticed the good voice and personal demeanor of a certain Muezzin Kamil Efendi who had been brought to his presence took him under his protection. He asked me to find him a good music teacher. I chose Ahmed Efendi who was truly a master of music and also played the ud very well. I sent the man to his yalı in Yeniköy. He approved of him. I asked that he be put on a salary and he accepted. He would go the yalı once a week and sometimes he call him to his and he would train Kamil. He taught him many works. Even after the martyrdom of the Pasha, his son Prince Sa'id Halim Bey who himself was a master musician, continued to pay the salary even under those conditions. He didn't have a good voice but the way he performed touched the spirit of the people listening even more than those with a good voice.

"(...) One evening when we returned home there was a dinner party for friends and a mevlud was performed. Although Ahmed Efendi was suffering from a stomach ailment, he performed masterfully. At the end there were very good fasıls.

"Ahmed Efendi, who spent the night at our house, wrote the following lines for the "Calligraphy Magazine" (Honorable Mahmud Kemal's love of music is without peer. 5 Rebiulahir 1339 Mevlevi Ahmed the son of Zekai Dede).

"He composed many songs from different makams. I asked Münir Bey who was the son of his sister where I could find his works. In his written reply he said, 'I guess that some of his works were put into notation by some people but like the works of his father his works were not noted by the conservatory and were not published. His library belongs to the family and is at Kurukavak

Music Teacher Hafız Ahmed and his class.

Street in Eyüp. His offspring won't touch it. I requested to look at them but I was not allowed. His son, Abdülhalim Bey, is a major at the NATO headquarters in İzmir. His wife and daughter are still living."

The above stories were written by İbnülemin Mahmut Kemal İnat.

The Problem of F

he changes in construction and form in Turkish classical music that became apparent toward the end of the 19th century are typical manifestations of the changes that were taking place in Ottoman society as a result of the strong winds blowing from the West. The old and classical music forms change and as a result, the rhythm of both music and life become faster. All aspects that affect music, from language and literature to social life, clearly show this change. A more fundamental change is the necessity of the writing down and recording of music in notation which up until that time had been memorized. This necessity is very important when the fact that numerous works have been lost due to the limitations of human memory. On the other hand, for those people who learned their music in the traditional meşk way, the disappearance of the master-student relationship, the impossibility of transmitting nuances in style and the absence of individual interpretation comprise the negative aspects of written notes. It has the effect of eliminating memory and shortening the difficult period of learning. More importantly, it limits individual contributions, the freedom of different interpretations which then brings forth standard performances and productions.

As the source closest to Zekai Dede, Hâfız Ahmed Efendi was a part of the "Determining and Organizing" Committee of Dârü'l-Elhan and instrumental in the recording in notes of hundreds of works that were in his memory.

During the period when Ottoman contacts with the West were intensifying and written notes were being used by the Royal Military Band, traditional music circles that had to live with these conflicts began to realize the necessity of adopting Western note-writing. This true transition period gather momentum toward the Republic with the inception of a new organization. The establishment of the "Dâru'l-Elhan" the first conservatory, was designed to record in written notes the works of masters that had survived to that day and thereby save them from possible oblivion. One of those musicians that took part in this effort from 1910 until his death is Hafız Ahmed Efendi. As the source closest to Zekai Dede, he was a part of the "Determining and Organizing" Committee of this foundation and instrumental in the recording in notes of hundreds of works that were in his memory.

In this way, the son of Zekai took his part in our musical history as one of the transmitters of past musical tradition of learning music by way of memorization to the modern times.

The following anecdote is frequently told to show his importance in this endeavor and his devotion to his own traditional values. "During the performance of the segah fasıl when a beste by Dellalzade was being sung, a disagreement over one note took place between Vezir Ziya Pasha, Director of the Conservatory, and the son of Zekai-zade. Ziya Pasha insisted that the note was an F sharp to which the son of Zekai objected. Hafız Ahmet Efendi resigned as a result, giving up his salary which amounted to ten gold pieces. His explanation of his resignation shows how fastidious and dedicated he was to the old values. This is what he said: 'My father rehearsed this work with Dellalzade himself and I rehearsed it with my father. My father warned me by saying "Watch it, Hafız, although it appears as an F sharp, it really is an F natural." If I render it as an F sharp, I would be disturbing the souls of both Dellalzade and my father, Zekai Dede"

OTTOMAN SOUNDS

Hacı Ârif Bey

1831 - 1885

Magnificent
Ottoman Composers

Hacı Arif Bey

acı Arif Bey is one, perhaps the first, of the most important composers of a form of music known as şarkı (song), examples of which began to appear during of the 19th century and which were composed under the influence of the classical form. The şarkı form is the counterpart in music of the social, political and cultural changes, in other words, modernization, that were taking place within the Ottoman Empire and during his lifetime. The modernization acts that appeared in various institutions of the Ottomans during the time of Selim III and Mahmut II brought with them as a "dissolution of the old order." From this viewpoint, Hacı Arif Bey is a Tanzimat musician committed to modernization. However, one should add that the şarkı form which in his hands matured through his efforts represents a transition. The wholeness of Hacı Arif Bey's şarkıs carefully maintains a balance between the classical style and the romantic style using a masterful melodic construction. The main theme of these songs is "love" combined with "melancholy" – a love that is more human than the love seen in older classical music pieces. This romantic opening that is represented by Felix Mendelssohn in Western music is known as the neo-classical period in the classification of Turkish music.

A life in reclusion, and a lonely death...

The man who became known as Hacı Arif Bey was born in 1831 in Eyüp as Mehmet Arif. His father was Ebubekir Efendi who was the secretary of the religious court in Eyüp. He was first noticed for the beauty of his voice when he was attending a school in Eyüp which at that time was an important cultural center where the upper class lived. He began taking music lessons from Zekai Efendi who was a bit older than he was and lived in the same district. This man who was to become a great musician and became known as Zekai Dede, started teaching him religious music and also introduced him to his own teacher, Eyyubi Mehmed Bey. As a result, Hacı Arif Bey became a student at the Muzıka-i Humayun (the Royal Military Band), got to know Dede Efendi and took the first serious steps for his musical education. After finishing school, he was appointed as a secretary in one of the offices of the Bab-ı Seraskeri (Ministry of Defense). Later when Sultan Abdülmecit heard and liked his voice, he was appointed to the Muzıka-i Humayun and there became a student of Haşim Bey. Dr. Suphi Ezgi states that "my master Zekai Efendi told me that Hacı Arif Bey learned 35 fasıls from Eyyubi Mehmed Bey. After this period, the mesks at the palace developed his talents further. Additionally, Abdülmecit appointed him as his own chamberlain.

Dede Efendi who listened to his voice when he was still a child immediately noticed his ability.

Hacı Arif Bey's fame increased after he had benefited a great deal from his lessons with Haşim Bey who was very impressed with the way he could memorize all the works that he taught him. During this time he in addition to his being a chamberlain and palace singer, was appointed as a music teacher to the talented palace concubines. In his work entitled "Harem", Çağatay Uluçay states that since this was a closed area, musical entertainment and musical meşks were given much importance and during the reigns of Abdülmecit, Abdülaziz, and Abdülhamit, the harem had quality musical ensembles.

This young man who had a beautiful voice and a good physical appearance became amorously involved with one of the concubines named Çeşm-i Dilber, He composed many songs for her, the most important of which is the one that starts with "The bruises of the arrows of your separation have passed." This affair became known in a very short time.

Sultan Abdülmecit, learning of this, gave his permission to marry this concubine, put him on a stipend, but asked him to leave the palace. This marriage lasted for 2 years, produced 2 sons. After the divorce he wanted to return to the palace and wrote a song dedicated to the Sultan in which he asked to be forgiven and be taken back into the palace.

After this event which was reported in an article written by Ali Riza Bey, the Minister of Fisheries, Hacı Arif Bey started a job at the Royal Military Band and music teaching in the harem, became involved with another concubine named Zülf-i Nigar and this relationship also resulted in marriage. Leaving the palace, Hacı Arif Bey moved to his mansion at Taşlık, and had a daughter. Shortly thereafter his second wife died of tuberculosis, affecting the composer very much. Some time later, Hacı Arif Bey, during the reign of Abdülaziz, had a similar adventure and married another concubine named Nigarnik. In the meantime, his fame had spread throughout the Empire and his works

numbered in the hundreds. He sold his place at Taşlık and bought himself a farm in Zincirliköyü. He started living here in solitude tending cows and sheep. It is not known when he went on pilgrimage and received the title Hacı (Pilgrim).

Hacı Arif Bey was appointed to the palace again during the reign of Sultan Abdülhamit II at a lower rank, and it has been reported that during this time he became irritable, was capricious, and had bouts of depression. His financial situation worsened and he started selling gifts

that had been given to him by the palace and his health deteriorated. He spent his time during the War of 1293! as a recluse, milking his cows totally oblivious to social life (during this period it is rumored that he grew a beard that came halfway down his chest). In 1885, at the age of 54, Hacı Arif Bey died in the arms of his son Cemil Bey after a heart attack at the Gümüşsuyu military barracks in a room of the Royal Military Band.

It is reported that there were only eleven people who attended his funeral. He is buried at the Yahya Efendi Cemetery in Beşiktaş.

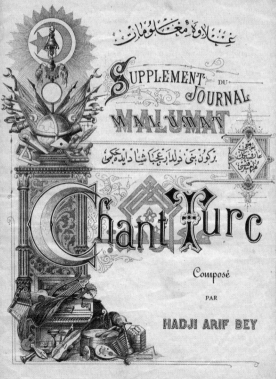

Hidden melancholy beneath a joyous mask...

acı Arif Bey, if one discounts the reign of Mahmut II during his childhood and Murat V who was the Sultan for only 3 months, lived through the reigns of Abdülmecit, Abdülaziz and Abdülhamit II. He is seen as a very famous, irreplaceable musician who had an off and on relationship with the palace.

During the period in which he was born into, Mahmut II, who himself was a great Turkish musician, protected this music, knew it very well but at the same time also contributed to the spread of Western music among the Ottomans. The traditional musicians of this period starting with Dede Efendi are: Dellalzade, Şakir Ağa, Kömürcüzade Hafız Efendi, Kazasker Mustafa Izzet Efendi, Numan Ağa, Zeki Mehmed Ağa. Turkish classical music, although showing some elements of modernization, had its golden age with all its traditional forms and styles.

Abdülmecit I, who succeeded his father Mahmut II, although he knew Western music very well, played the piano, and was a Sultan who put into effect many reforms, nevertheless was very much interested in Hacı Arif Bey. When Hacı Arif Bey was a very young and inexperienced singer attending the Royal Military Band, the Sultan listened to him and gave him a job as one of his chamberlains. Hacı Arif Bey at that time was 8 years younger than the Sultan and was about 19 or 20 years old.

Hacı Ârif Bey

This distinguished position resulted in his getting a lot of respect and his fame to spread. He composed songs one after the other and became a teacher to the concubines in the Royal Harem.

The Ottoman Empire under the reign of Abdülmecit I entered the Tanzimat period with the Imperial Decree of Gülhane. Imperial reform edicts were published and as a result there were developments in the fields of law and education. It was during this period that the Ministry of General Education was founded, the first high school for girls, a war academy, a school for civil servants and a school for telegraphy were opened. The operation of Şirket-I Hayriye ferry boats, the building Galata Bridge, the Mecidiye Barracks, and Dolmabahçe Palace, the first private newspaper (Tercüman-ı Ahval), and the printing of paper money were all developments during the reign of Abdülmecit I.

He caused quite a stir when he attended the grand ball given by the French ambassador in 1856. Up until that time, the sultans attending a ball was unseeming. Additionally he wore jewels on his labels and also displayed the Legion of Honor which had been accepted by an Ottoman sultan for the first time.

This 22-year reign of this Tanzimat Sultan can be said to be the best part of Hacı Arif Bey's life. Because of his amorous affairs, he left the palace twice and came back twice, but music and his compositions were instrumental in his ups and downs during this time. He proclaimed his love through his songs, he declared his sorrows through his songs and asked for forgiveness through his songs by winning the heart of the Sultan came back to the palace.

Hacı Arif Bey was demoralized by the death of Sultan Abdülmecit from tuberculosis at the age of 38. He had a more formal relationship with Sultan Abdülaziz who then ascended the throne. He continued to produce more mature compositions during the reign (which lasted 15 years) of Sultan

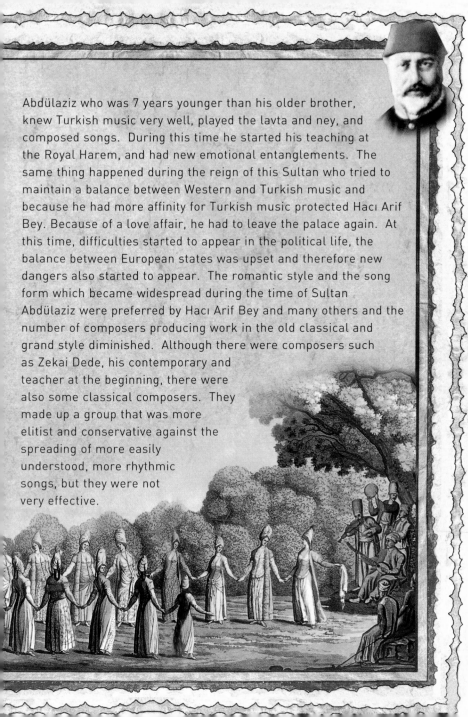

Abdülaziz who was 7 years younger than his older brother, knew Turkish music very well, played the lavta and ney, and composed songs. During this time he started his teaching at the Royal Harem, and had new emotional entanglements. The same thing happened during the reign of this Sultan who tried to maintain a balance between Western and Turkish music and because he had more affinity for Turkish music protected Hacı Arif Bey. Because of a love affair, he had to leave the palace again. At this time, difficulties started to appear in the political life, the balance between European states was upset and therefore new dangers also started to appear. The romantic style and the song form which became widespread during the time of Sultan Abdülaziz were preferred by Hacı Arif Bey and many others and the number of composers producing work in the old classical and grand style diminished. Although there were composers such as Zekai Dede, his contemporary and teacher at the beginning, there were also some classical composers. They made up a group that was more elitist and conservative against the spreading of more easily understood, more rhythmic songs, but they were not very effective.

"In the arts there can be no royal decree."

bdülhamid II who was the second son of Sultan Abdülmecit was the 34th Sultan of the Ottomans between the years 1876 and 1909. This 30- year period was praised as the period of Devr-i Hamidi "Hamid's Period", while it was also criticized as Devr-i İstibdat "Period of Oppression" by the intellectuals and opposition members. It is pointed out that there was not such a warm relationship between Hacı Arif Bey and this Sultan who learned his music from two Italians, Guatelli and Lombardi, who were with the Royal Military Band. Certain incidents that have been reported showed the interesting part of this period. For example, a song that was composed by Hacı Arif Bey that started with the line, "I am a wandering lover whose star has fallen." The word "ahter" which means star in Persian, was thought to refer to the Yıldız Palace. This word was changed to "talih" which means fortune. Again in the same song, the words of the poet "To whom should I entreat, my Sultan, while you are there" was changed from my "Sultan" was changed to my "şive kar" (coquettish sweetheart).

The reply that Hacı Arif Bey, even though he was not feeling well, gave to the Sultan who wanted him to perform in his presence was very courageous. Rıfat Bey, who relayed the Sultan's message to Hacı Arif Bey, upon receiving the reply that the master was not feeling well, relayed it to the Sultan as if Hacı Arif Bey were being capricious. Incensed the Sultan said, "If he is sick, what is he doing at the Royal Band? Bring him here immediately." Hacı Arif Bey again refused by saying, "In the arts there can be no royal decree." Not only did he refuse to go but also reminded the Sultan who was 11 years younger than he that when he was holding the Sultan in his lap as a baby, the Sultan wet himself." Whereupon the Sultan ordered him to be kept in his room at the Royal Band. It is said that he was released from confinement 50 days later for the sake of the song which is mentioned above.

One of the Western style music teachers of the Royal Band, Zati Bey (Arca), relates that although Abdülhamit was not as fond of ala turka (Turkish music) as some of the other sultans, he liked Hacı Arif Bey's songs and the way he sang them. According to some other sources, the famous segah song which Hacı Arif Bey composed upon the death of his second wife which started with the words "There is no medicine for my bosom which has broken into a hundred pieces" was actually a song that was composed for Vehice Sultan who was one of Abdülhamit's daughters. According to this source, for his daughter who died of tuberculosis, the Sultan gave Namık Kemal's poem to Hacı Arif Bey to compose.

Abdülhamit II

"What a voice that was"

Hacı Arif Bey who first comes to mind as a composer in the song form had, as is shown in many sources, a beautiful voice and was once one of the best and most famous singers of his time. İbnülemin Mahmut Kemal Bey is one of the many people who had listened to him and conveyed their impressions. We can also see this in other sources that he had a wonderful voice Hoş Sada (Pleasant Sound). In his Istanbul Encyclopedia which is a comprehensive publication about Istanbul, starting in 1944, Reşat Ekrem Koçu states the following: "My teacher, İbnülemin Mahmud Kemal, during his childhood, had the opportunity to listen to Hacı Arif Bey during a mevlid performed by his neighbor, Fındık Hafız 'What a voice that was.' Singing together with his friends his voice dominated the others. Even though 60 years have passed, I can still hear the beauty of that voice. Musical masters noticed the beauty of his voice at a very young age."

Mehmet Sadi Bey

Mehmet Sadi Bey who wrote the words of many of Hacı Arif Bey's songs was a poet who had a handwritten "Divan" entitled "Gülşen-i Asar" (Remains of the Rose Garden) and one of Hacı Arif Bey's closest friends. Many of the best-known composers, singers and instrument players took part in musical discussions and fasıls that were held in his mansion in Çengelköy. With Hacı Arif Bey heading the list, these were Şevki Bey, Şekerci Cemil Bey, Tanburi Ali Efendi, Rıfat and Hacı Faid Bey and belonging to the younger generation, Tanburi Cemil Bey, Rahmi Bey, Rauf Yekta Bey, Nevres Bey and Ahmet Rasim Bey. It is rumored that he had a special place on a sofa in the largest public room furnished lavishly with satin mattresses and carpet pillows overlooking "Marika's Garden." There was a sleeping room in the selamlık section of the mansion especially reserved for Hacı Arif Bey who spent most of his nights there. He regularly attended the Friday gatherings and many other nights at the mansion.

Sadi Yaver Ataman relates the following anecdote: "Both Hacı Arif Bey and Şevki Bey used to perform their new compositions during these meetings. My father used to remark that Hacı Arif Bey had a deep bass and throaty, beautiful voice. Mehmet Sadi Bey is the author of the poems which Hacı Arif Bey, whose life had its ups and downs, whose social life and status varied from rich and respected to poor and lonely, found reflection of his natural inclinations and understanding of art in. They were kindred spirits and carried this to their private lives."

Hikmet Feridun Es, in one of the serial articles he published in Akşam (a daily newspaper) in 1949, relates the following anecdote:

"Mehmet Sadi Bey towards the end of one of the gatherings, recited his poem which started with the line: 'It is wrong to remember beauties as unfaithful' so that he could compose a song.

"The composer who was in a hurry, retired to his chambers and began to compose in the Hicaz Makam. But because of the nature of the makam, the poem needed additional lines. Trusting to his special relationship with the poet, he could not wait till morning and grabbing the candle he went to the "harem" section and banged on the door waking the people who had been on their feet till the small hours of the night. Servinaz Bacı answered the door and asked who it was and informed him that the master had retired. Hacı Arif Bey said 'Go and fetch Mehmet Bey.'

"After some hesitation, aware of the special relationship the two men had, she said, 'One moment please,' and fetched Mehmet Bey.

Mehmet Bey appeared a short while later with a shawl over his night shirt, smiling he said 'Well, sir what can I do for you?' Hacı Arif Bey replied, 'Sir, I am sorry to disturb you, I set your poem to music but I need some additional lines to complete it.' Mehmet Sadi Bey, extremely delighted that one of his poems had been composed, squatted on the floor and in candlelight added the following lines: "If you want to reach union like Sadi, you should persevere so that you reach your goal." This incident took place in 1879 and the above lines constitute the beginning of the second hicaz song in the musemmen usul."

His Musicianship and Works

Hacı Arif Bey, who was closer to lyricism than to the classical form and mysticism, gave the song form a permanent and perfect individual content. Prince Sa'it Halim Pasha, a statesman who was very much interested in music and very knowledgeable about music, said, "Songs become songs after Hacı Arif Bey. Before him they were bestes!" Rauf Yekta Bey states that no other composer during his time was as productive and Suphi Ezgi states that he composed songs in a gentle and brilliant manner.

The fact that he started very early in life, that he had a very strong musical memory and that his accumulation of knowledge was expansive, resulted in his composing many and well structured songs. Many sources report that he composed very quickly. For example, one of his students, Leon Hancıyan, relates that one night when Hacı Arif Bey was somewhat depressed, he composed eight songs, one after the other. Another story relates that when Sultan Abdülaziz sent him a poem to compose, he composed seven songs all in different makams. It is very important that in a period of decline in classical Turkish music, a composer of the caliber of productivity of Hacı Arif Bey should appear. Furthermore, due to his fame and stature and the strength of his students, this tradition of music was further developed. It is safe to say that none of the composers that followed him were free of the influence of this romantic tradition.

Although he had a very solid understanding of classical music, he composed songs, in his words "in a new vein." This was entirely due to the tumultuous and sentimental nature of his inner being. He was not concerned with the academic side of music, composed as he felt but did not ignore the fundamentals of musicology. The works that he left behind are still enjoyed by people from all walks of life due to the richness of rhythm and melodic color. The human element that reflects the man in his works still appeals to many. Ruşen Ferit Kam states "Hacı Arif Bey is a peerless artist who through his songs takes us to the depths of imagination which reflect his power of genius. Even in the most joyful of his songs, there is an element of melancholy."

Historian İsmail Hami Danişmend says "This great man is a very important personage in our classical period due to his influence and the new paths he has opened in our musical history. The fact that three sultans from Sultan Mecid to Sultan Hamid protected him and put up with his caprices is a testimony to his importance." This is an interesting observation from a field outside of music.

The influence of his music has reverberated throughout our musical history through the efforts of his students headed by Şevki Bey, Kanuni Mehmet Bey, Santuri Ethem Efendi, Leon Hancıyan, Zati Arca, Hanende Şeyh Servet Efendi, Firiftzen Asım Bey, even Bimen Şen. He reorganized the kürdilihicazkar makam and composed many songs in that makam. Additionally he is the founder of the usul called "müsemmen" which has been used extensively since.

He has only one composition in the grand form (nihavend makam, a beste without chorus) and eight religious ilahis that have survived to this day. One of his students, Servet Efendi, claims that he had 1000 compositions, 386 of which were put into notes. He wrote a book entitled "Mecmua-i Arifi" in 1873 which contained songs of other composers as well as how own and had it printed. Some of his other works are: "Meyhane mi bu, bezm-i tarabhane-i Cem mi," "Is this a drinking house or is it the drinking society of Cem?" "İftirakındır sebep bu nale vü feryadıma," "ıt is separation from you that causes my screams and whinings." Kurdu meclis aşıkan meyhanede," "The lovers gathered at the drinking house," "Çözülme zülfüne ey dil-ruba...," "Don't let down your hair, oh beloved," "Düşer mi şanına ey şeh-i huban" "Does it become your fame, the queen of beauties?" and "Esti nesim-l nev-bahar" "The wind of spring has blown."

A Student of His: Lem'i Atlı

*L*em'i Atlı, who lived between 1869 and 1945, is a major composer who made the transition from the Ottoman Empire to the Republic. He became Hacı Arif Bey's student at the age of 14. He is an important link in the chain which can be characterized as "song composition" and which began and expanded with Hacı Arif Bey and continued with Şevki Bey. Atlı who learned a lot from his teacher and was encouraged by him to compose songs, in a book he published under the name of "Memoirs" related how he met him and how they worked together. This relationship lasted until Hacı Arif Bey's death (two years later).

Mevlevis and Mevlevi Ayins

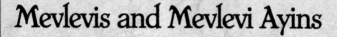

The most widespread "tarikat" (religious order) that combined music with religion and that gave an important role to music in worship is the Mevlevi Order. The mevlevis who achieved great progress in music, especially in the 19th century, used musical instruments in their religious ceremonies and together with the recital of ilahis and the rendition of musical works in the grand order called "ayins," performed religious dances called "sema." Sema is a difficult dance. It is said that the mevlevis attain a fluid and harmonious dance style only by securing a foot on a nail and doing the meşk for months. Since the dance is not a form of entertainment, it is not forbidden by Islam and there are numerous books on the merits of this dance. At the mevlevi lodges, tarikat ayins are called "mukabele;" the place where the sema takes place is called "semahane;" the players and

singers are "mutriban;" and the raised platform where they sit is called "mutribhane." "Semazenbaşı (Head Semazen) directs the sema ceremony. The mukabele starts with the recital of the "Na't-ı Şerif (Sacred Eulogy of the Prophet) by the "naathan" (na't singer). This composition by Itri is followed by a ney taksim (instrumental improvisation). The "sikke" (hat) on the semazens' heads symbolizes gravestones, the "hırka" (cloak) they wear symbolizes graves and the "tennure" (skirts), their shrouds.

The mevlevi ayins are monumental works of Turkish music. Important composers such as Itri, Dede Efendi, Selim III, Zekai Dede are examples. There are 46 ayins that have survived to the present. Many important works have appeared about mevlevi music and mevlevi ayins. The written notes of all the ayins were published by the Istanbul Municipality Conservatory Classification Committee through the special efforts of Rauf Yekta Bey and Zekai-zade Ahmed Efendi. Abdülbaki Gölpınarlı who has done serious research on the Mevlevis and Sufism has this to say in his book "Mevlevis after Mevlana" (Istanbul, 1983 p. 464): "What is mevlevi music? What is its specialty in that music which we call classical music? What has it given to that music and what has it taken from it? The answers to all these questions would make a book. To answer them and to give opinions on these matters is beyond my authority. I am simple putting it forth. Halil Dikmen, may his soul rest in peace, wrote a book about mevlevi music and I am waiting for its publication." The article in part is as follows: "Mevlevi ayins which are a part of our religious music because of the breadth of their construction are monumental works. Four selams that make up the ayin consist of instrumental refrains which are tied together. The third selam also has a vocal section. Religious and non-religious works have different makams. In addition, religious works have differences in their performances within themselves. They are made up of durak, ayin and ilahi.

"Mevlevi ayins according to their selams have been composed in relatively long usul as well as short usul such as: devr-i kebir and frenkçin. Where the beat is heavy or quick, the distribution of the notes over the syllables of the musical text, the length of the melody that syllables of the text would indicate, the organization of this melody makes up the tavır of the ayin. It is very important for the ayin singers to understand this point and not sing the ayin as an ilahi. The head ney player directs the singing group as a whole. The ayin singers sing the ayin by using two or three kudums for marking the beat. The usul of ayins is velvele which is special to mevlevi ayins.

"The ayins are started by the singing of Itri's famous na't by one person. After this the chief ney player does an improvisation which shows what makam is to follow and after that a peşrev called a "devr" and which is composed in the devr-i kebir usul is presented. Since with this peşrev the "devr-i Veledi" will be finished, the sheikh starts to walk to his post. The distance is six steps and while he is walking this distance, the head ney player does another short improvisation which shows the progress of the makam again. Then the selams with their refrains are performed. A short while after the start of the third selam, while the ayin has reached the top of its ecstasy a yürük semai starts and gets faster and faster. The fourth selams are always composed in the evfer usul in order to bring back serenity and peace.

"In these selams melody and usul are combined with great expertise. The reading part of the ayin is finished with the reading in the fourth selam which is followed by a last peşrev which follows a fast peşrev composed in the düyek usul. A last short yürük semai is performed by neys which is followed by another ney improvisation and then the ayin is over.

"When speaking of mevlevi music in connection with ayins, it is necessary to point out that the free and wide use of music by the mevlevis has made a great contribution to secular music performed outside of the lodges. This is clearly shown by the fact that most of the masterpieces in our musical repertoire were the works of composers belonging to the Mevlevi Religious Order. The Mevlevi lodges have been the institutions which have been instrumental in the development of composers whose work we still admire. The Mevlevi lodges were places where music in its purest form was taught and performed, contrary to type of music that was in vogue at the palace.

"As a result of this, it is natural to notice a great affinity in taste between mevlevi music and secular music. Even though duraks and ilahis have their own form, the wider spirit of the ayins shows their influence in some bestes and even some şarkıs. In short, one can feel the influence of bestes when listening to songs, and the influence of ayins when listening to bestes."

Index of Terms

Ayin
Mevlevi order – music played during worship.

Ayinhan
Mevlevi order – singer in a religious service

Bayram
religious festival

Beste
a vocal composition consisting of four verses each followed by the same melodic passage

Çile
mystic orders – period of forty days during which a novice has to fast and engage in religious exercises before admission to an order of dervishes

Dede
mystic orders – sheikh

Devr
1) rhythmic cycle; 2) a ritual whirling

Divan
a poet's collected poems arranged alphabetically

Durak
a form in Turkish religious music, tonic note.

Evher
rhythmic pattern of 9 beats used especially Mevlevi music.

Fasıl
a concert program all in the same makam

Ferahnak
a compound makam a century and a half old

Gazel
extemporaneous vocal taksim

Hafız
one who knows the whole Koran by memory

Hamam
public Turkish bath

Harem
women's apartments

Hırka
dervish's cloak

Hoca
Muslim teacher

Islahat
imperial reform edicts

İlâhî
hymn

İmam
prayer leader

Lavta
an instrument like the ud, now out of use.

Kar
a form; the first piece sung after the peşrev in a classical fasıl

Kaside
eulogy or commemorative poem put to music and considered as religious music.

Kıta
piece of poetry of two or more couplets, complete in itself as to idea.

Köçekçe
tune or music used while a man is dancing.

Kudum
a small double drum used for rhythm in Mevlemi music; it is played with special small sticks.

Makam
a concept of melodic creation which determines tonal relations, tessitura, starting tone, reciting tone and the finalis, as well as an overall indication of the melodic contour and patterns. Its closest counterpart in Western music is the medieval concept of mode. Examples of different makams are: suzidilara, rast-i ceded, hicazeyn, şevk-ı dil, arazbar buselik, neva kürdi, gerdaniye kürdı, hüseyni zemzeme, şevkutarab kürdilihicazkar

Mescid
small mosque

Meşk
musical rehearsal

Meşkane
school of music

Mevlevi
member of the order of dervishes founded by Mevlana Jalaladdin Rumi, called also the "whirling dervishes."

Mevlevi ayini
vocal composition of four parts, accompanying the ceremony performed by the Mevlevi dervishes.

Mevlevihane
lodge of Mevlevi dervishes

Mevlid, mevlud
a religious meeting held in memory of a deceased person in which the Mevlud is chanted.

Mevlidhan
head chanter of the Mevlud

Muamma
riddle whose solution depends on changing the letters in a key word.

Mukabele
mystic orders – ceremony of whirling or zikr

Murabba
a makam used in old times; the old name of the beste composition form.

Müzika-i Humayun
the Royal Military Band

Naat or Na't
a poem praising the Prophet Muhammad; eulogy

Ney
a reed flute played especially in Mevlevi music

Nizam-ı Cedid
the new system inaugurated by Sultan Selim III; especially, the new regular troops then organized.

Perde
note; the pitch of a note

Peşrev
the best-known form of music, usually of four parts, used with long rhythmic patterns and played at the beginning of a classical music performance.

Savt
a form used in religious music by certain orders.

Selamlık
the part of a large Muslim house reserved for males.

Sema
a whirling dance performed during a Mevlevi service

Semahane
dervish meeting house for religious music and whirling

Semai
a rhythmic pattern with three beats; a form special to vocal music; a form used by minstrels in folk music

Semazen
a Mevlevi who performs the sema

Sikke
a headdress special to any dervish order

Sufi
mystic; devotee, pertaining to a devotee or dervish

Şarkı
song (the most common secular vocal form).

Şeyh
head of a religious order; sheikh.

Taksim
an instrumental improvisation

Tanbur
any string instrument played by plucking.

Tanzimat
the political reforms of Abdülmecid in 1839 and the period following

Tarih
chronogram

Tarih düşürmek
to compose a chronogram

Tarikat
religious order, order of dervishes.

Tavır
deviating realization of a melodic line.

Tekke
dervish lodge

Tennure
a wide skirt worn by the Mevlevi dervishes

Tevşih
a form in religious music

Türkü
folk song

Usul
rhythmic pattern, rule which regulates the metric structure of a composition

Velvele
Subdividing the beats of a rhythmic pattern to make a more complex pattern.

Yürük sema'i
1) a rhythmic pattern with 6 beats; 2) a form of vocal music sung just before the instrumental piece at the end of a fasıl.

Zemin
the music of the first line of a song.

Zencir
the longest rhythmic pattern, with 120 beats.

Zikr
dervish religious service; litany